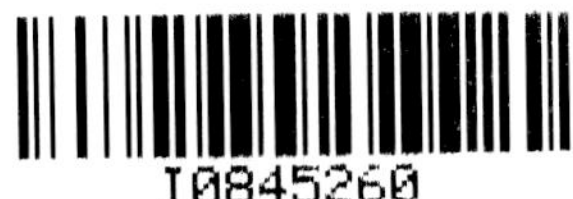

this belongs to

____

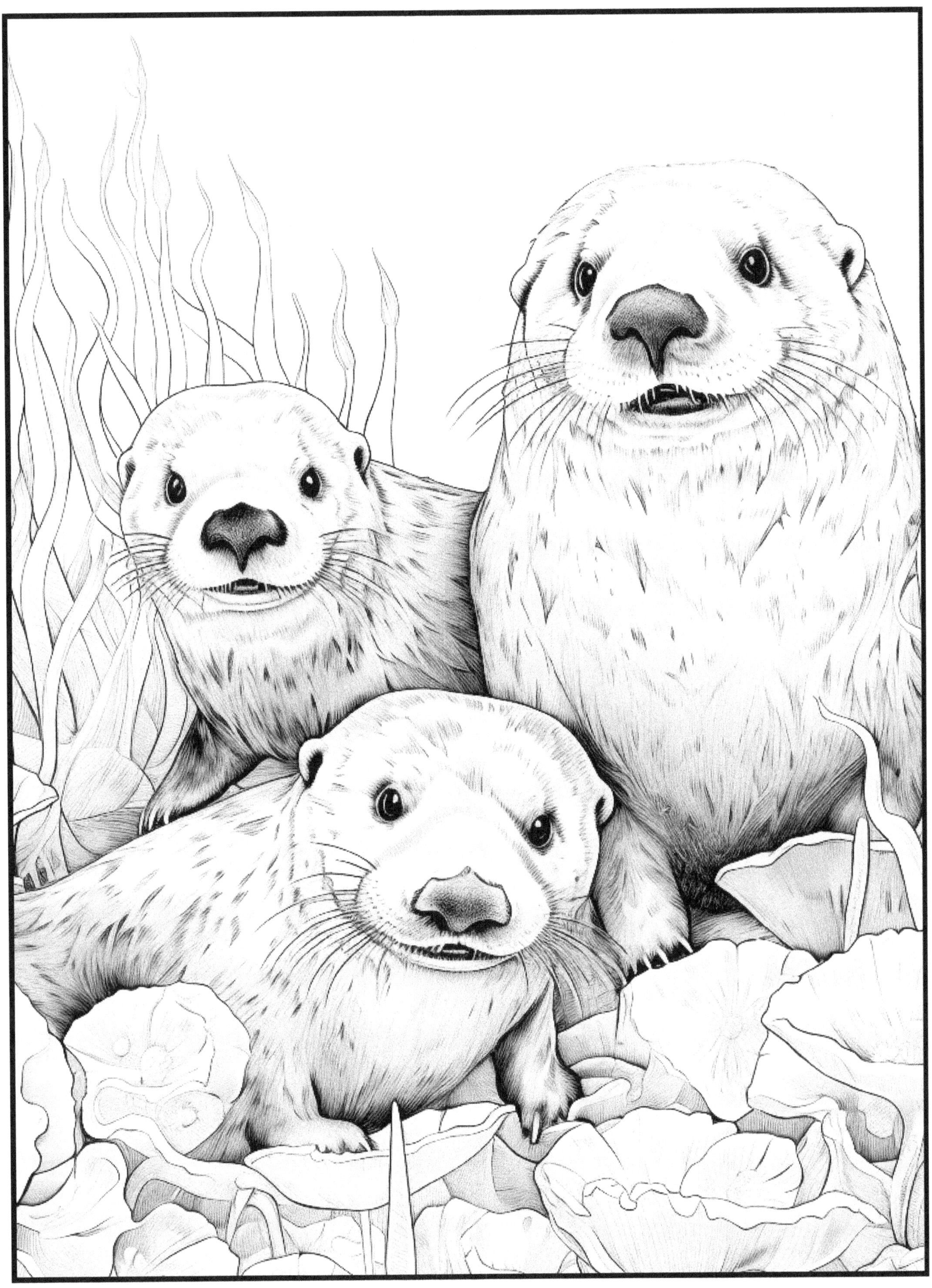

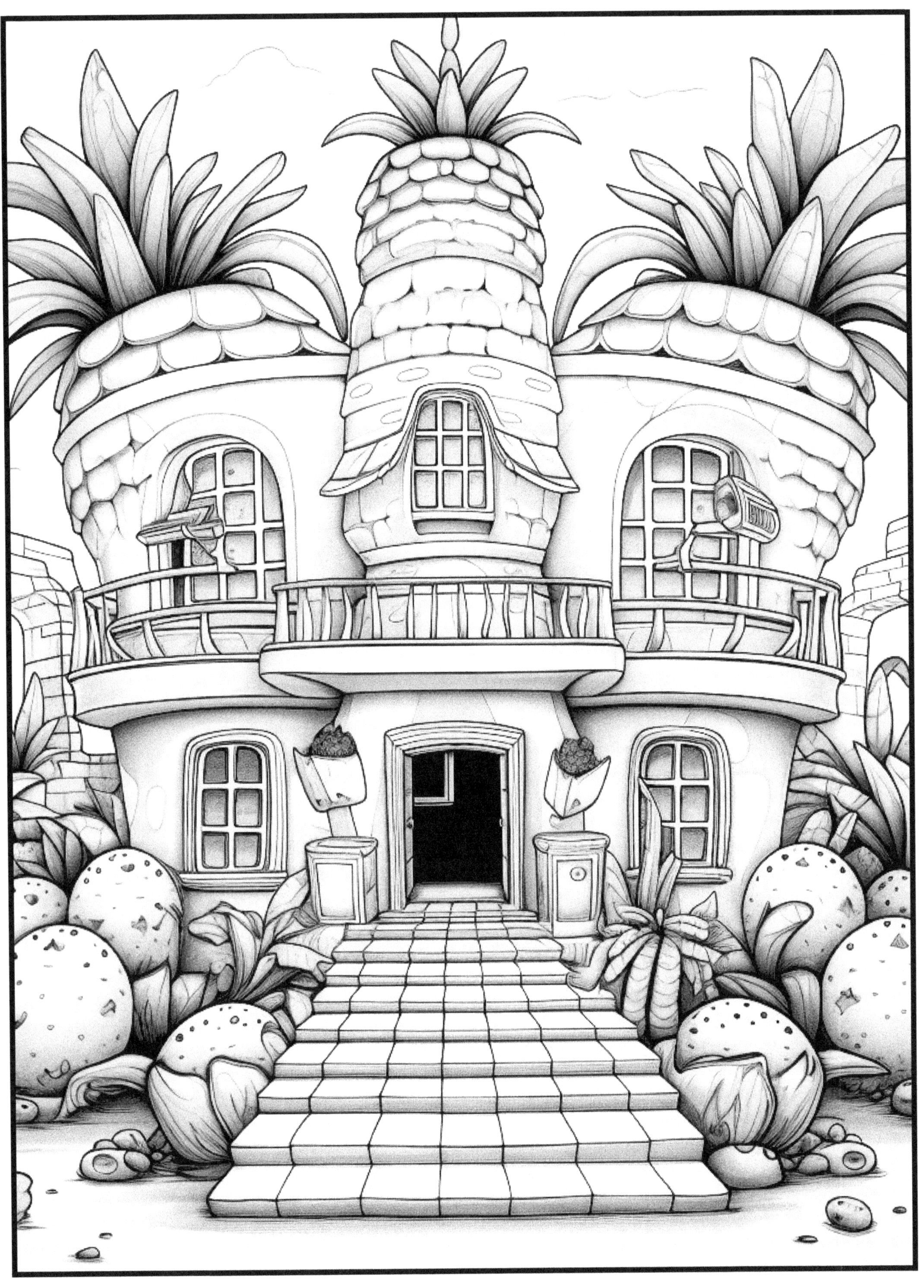

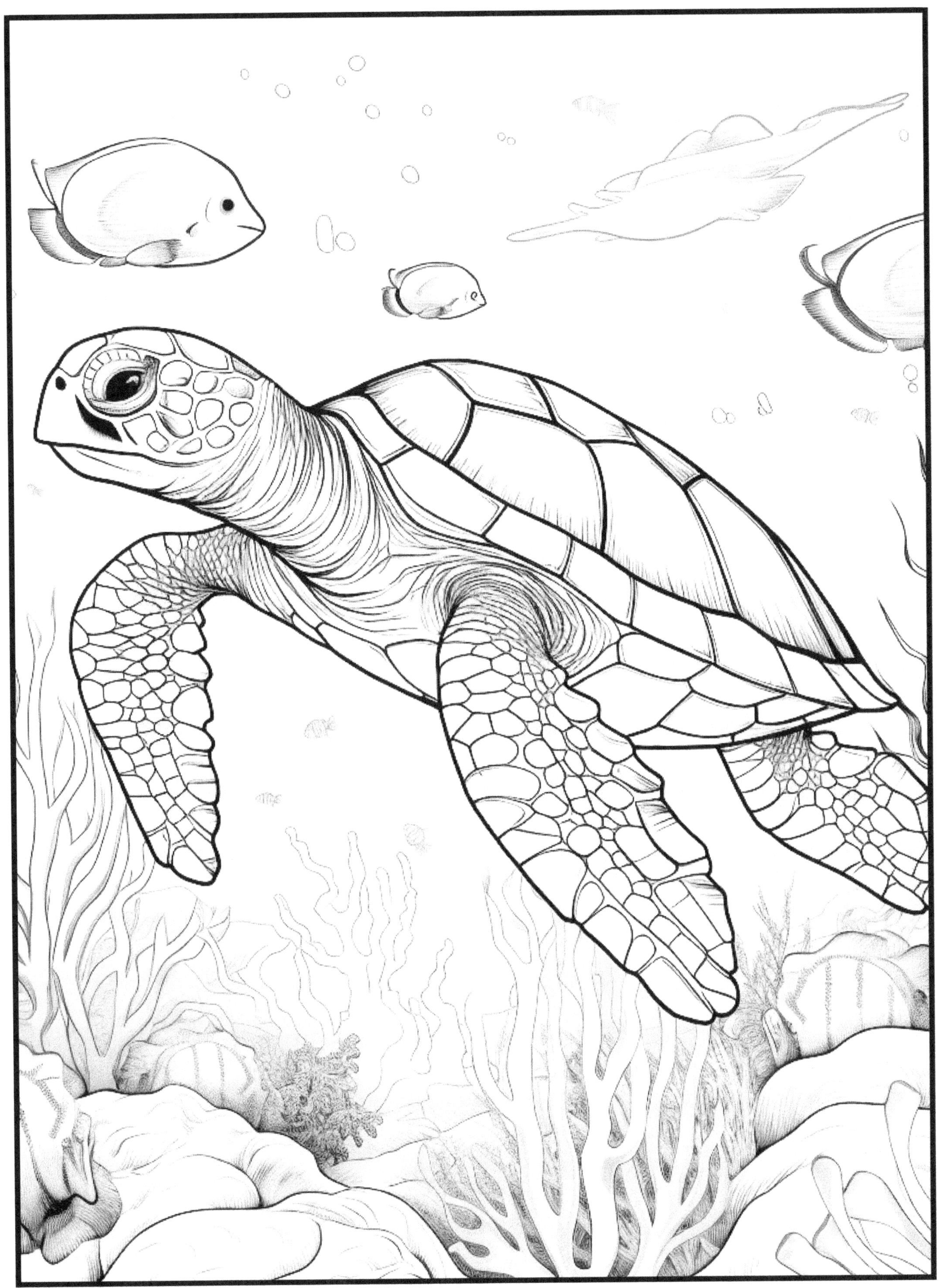

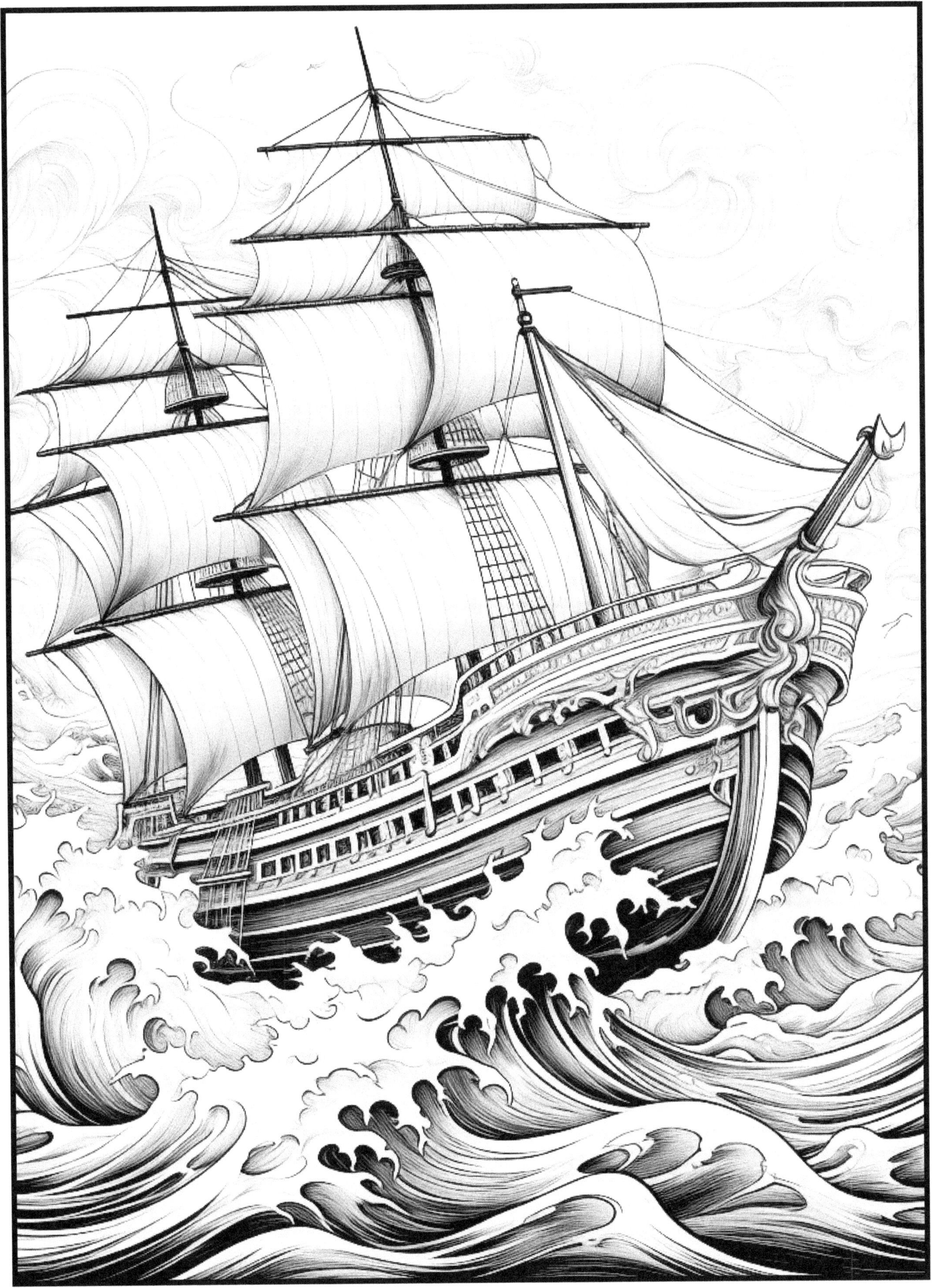

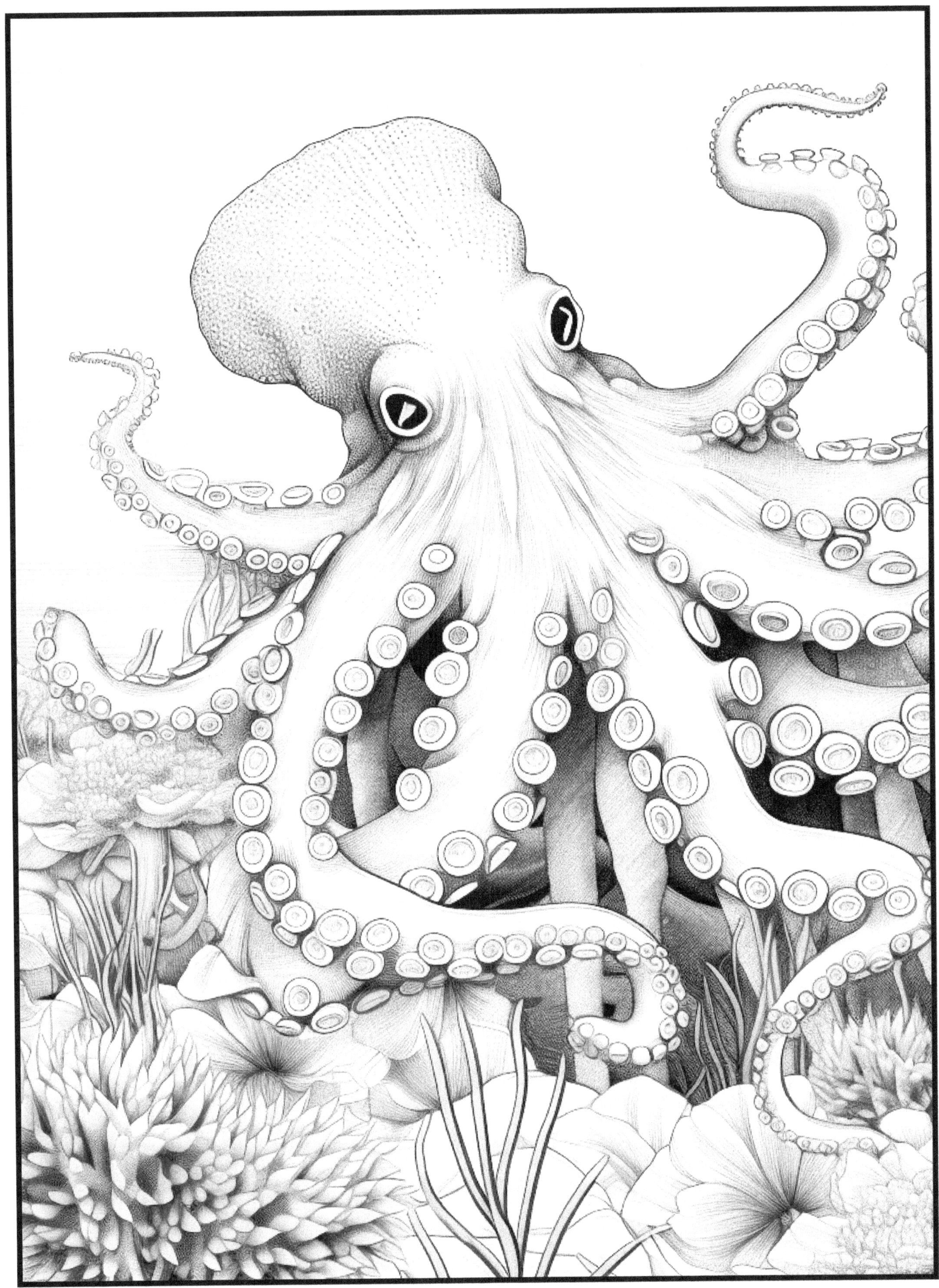

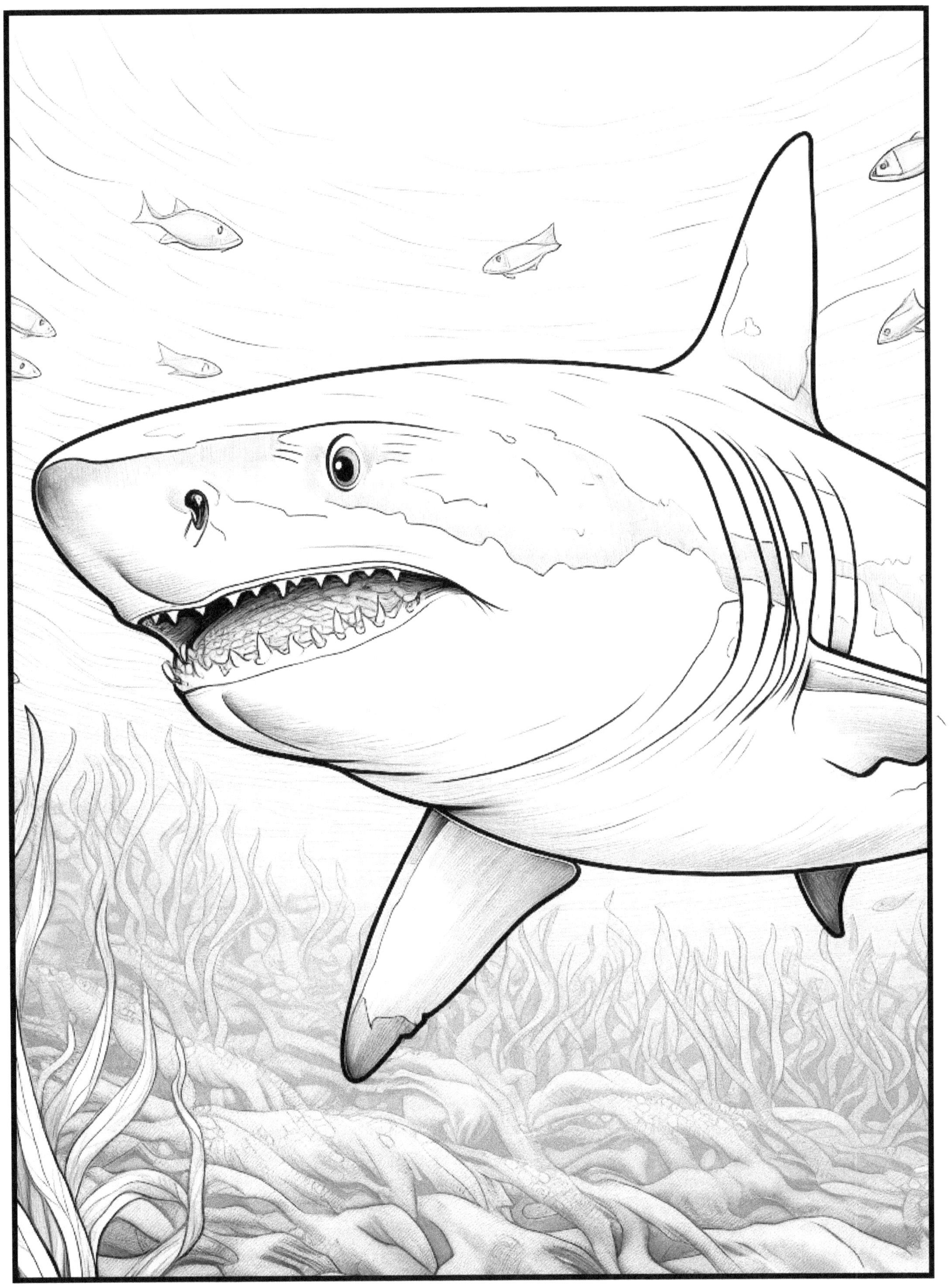

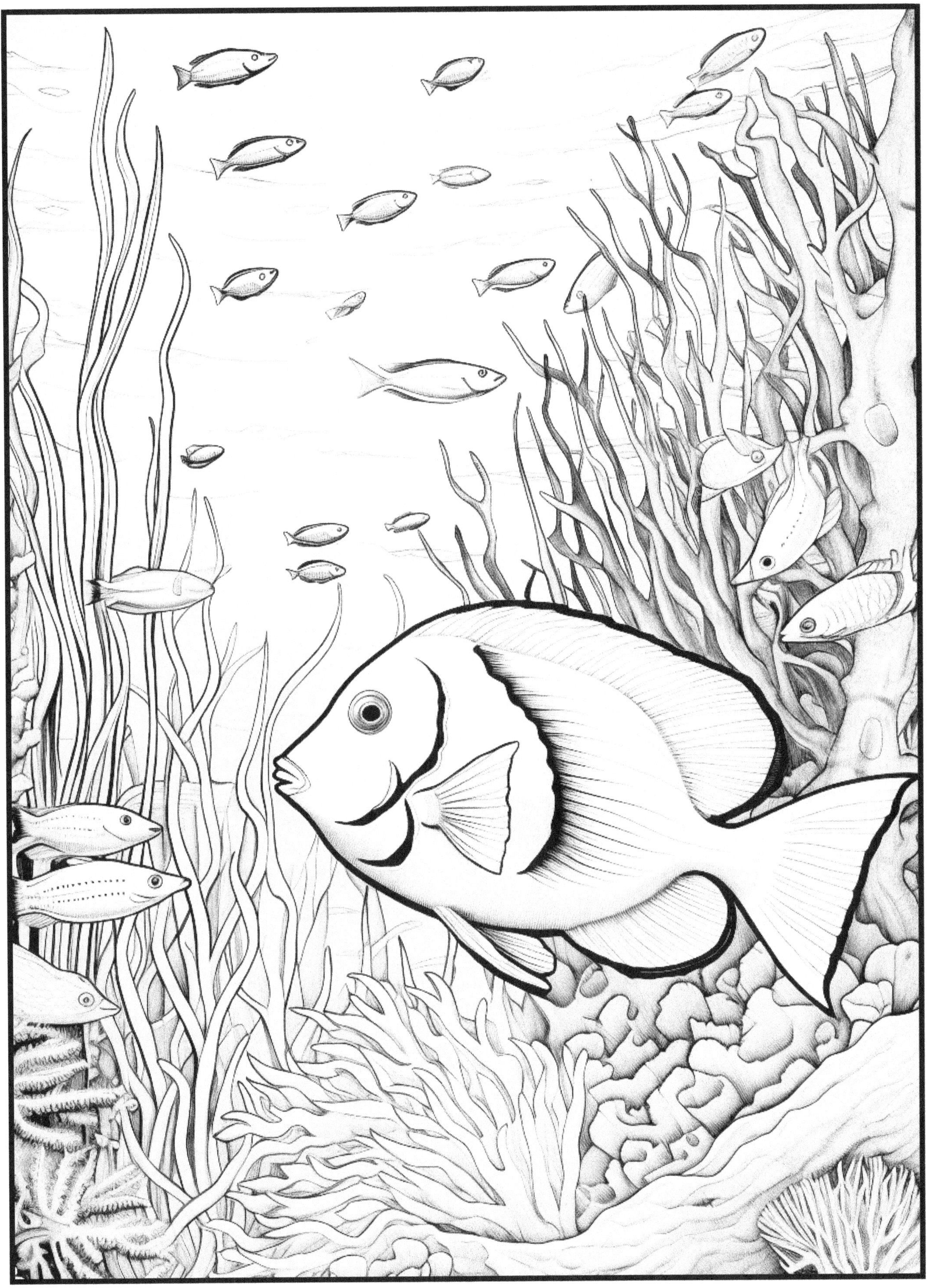

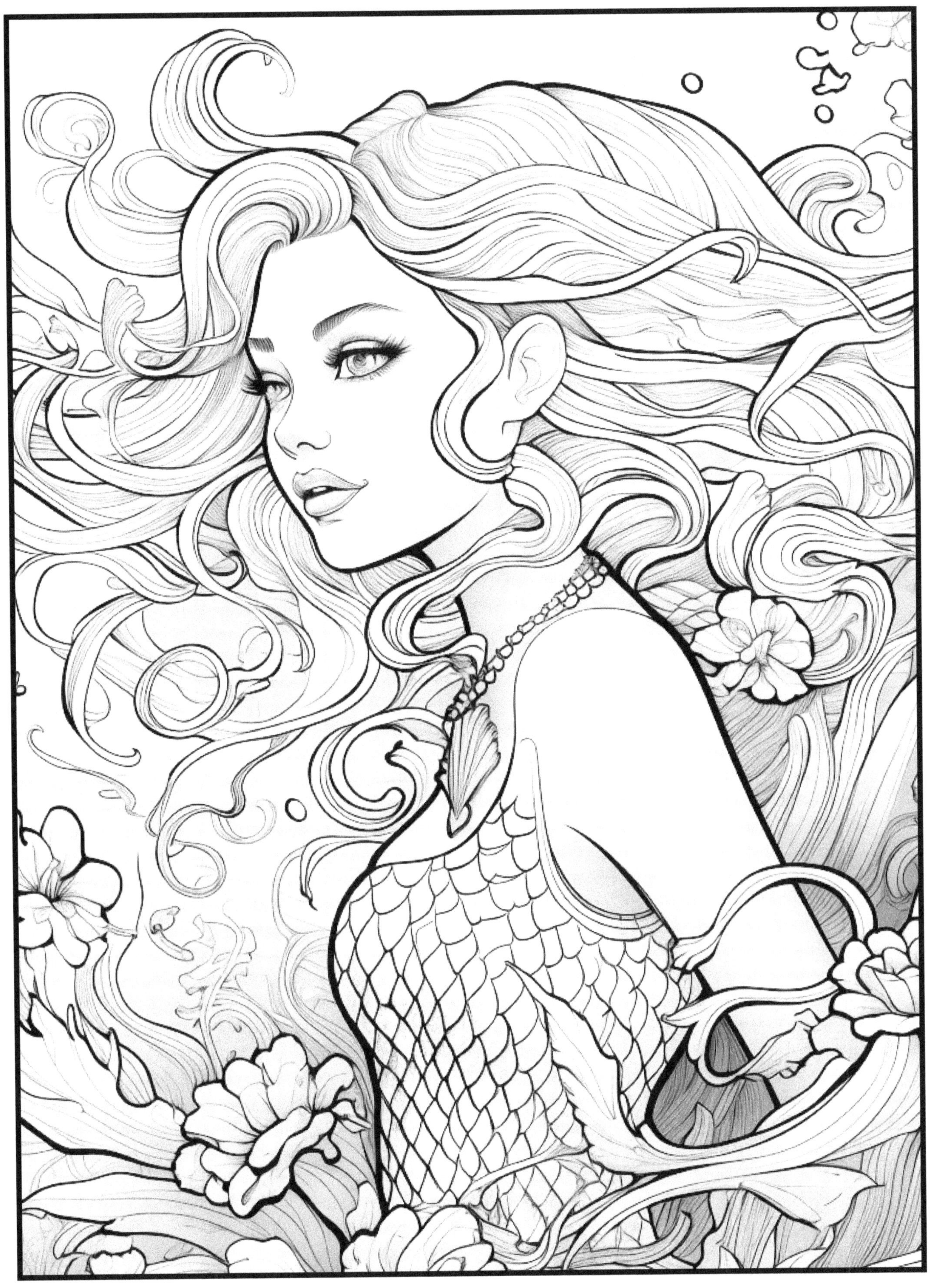

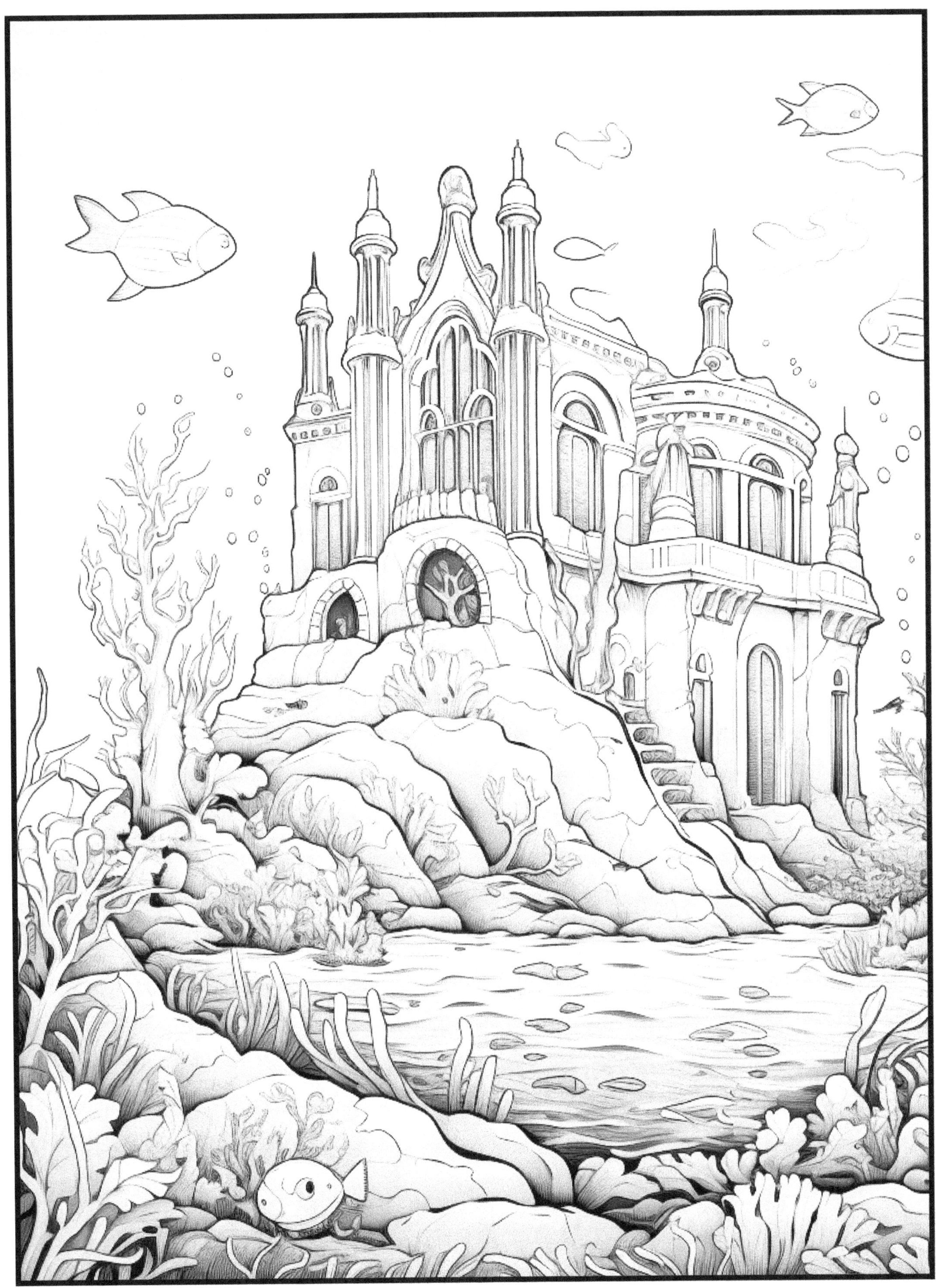

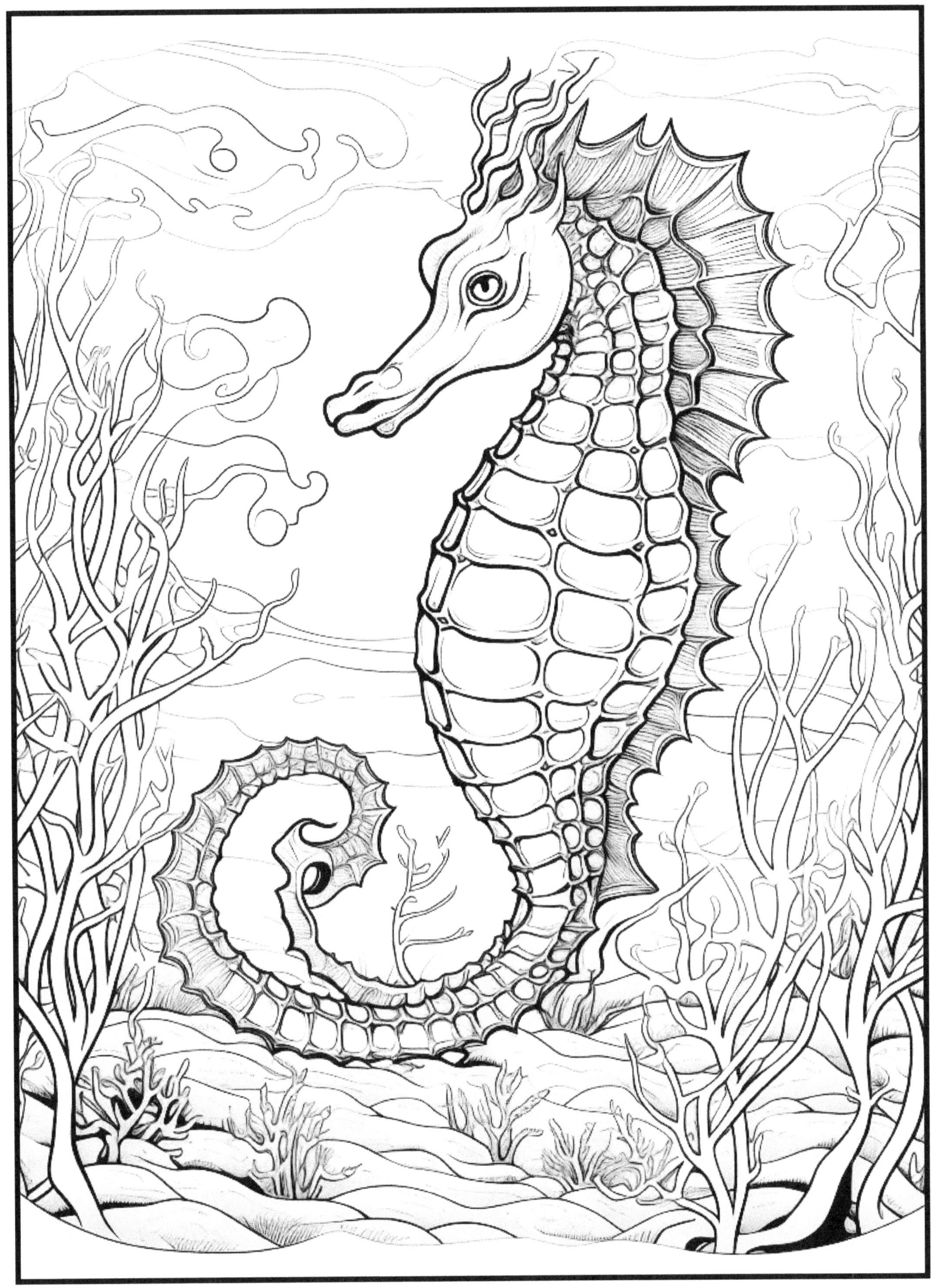

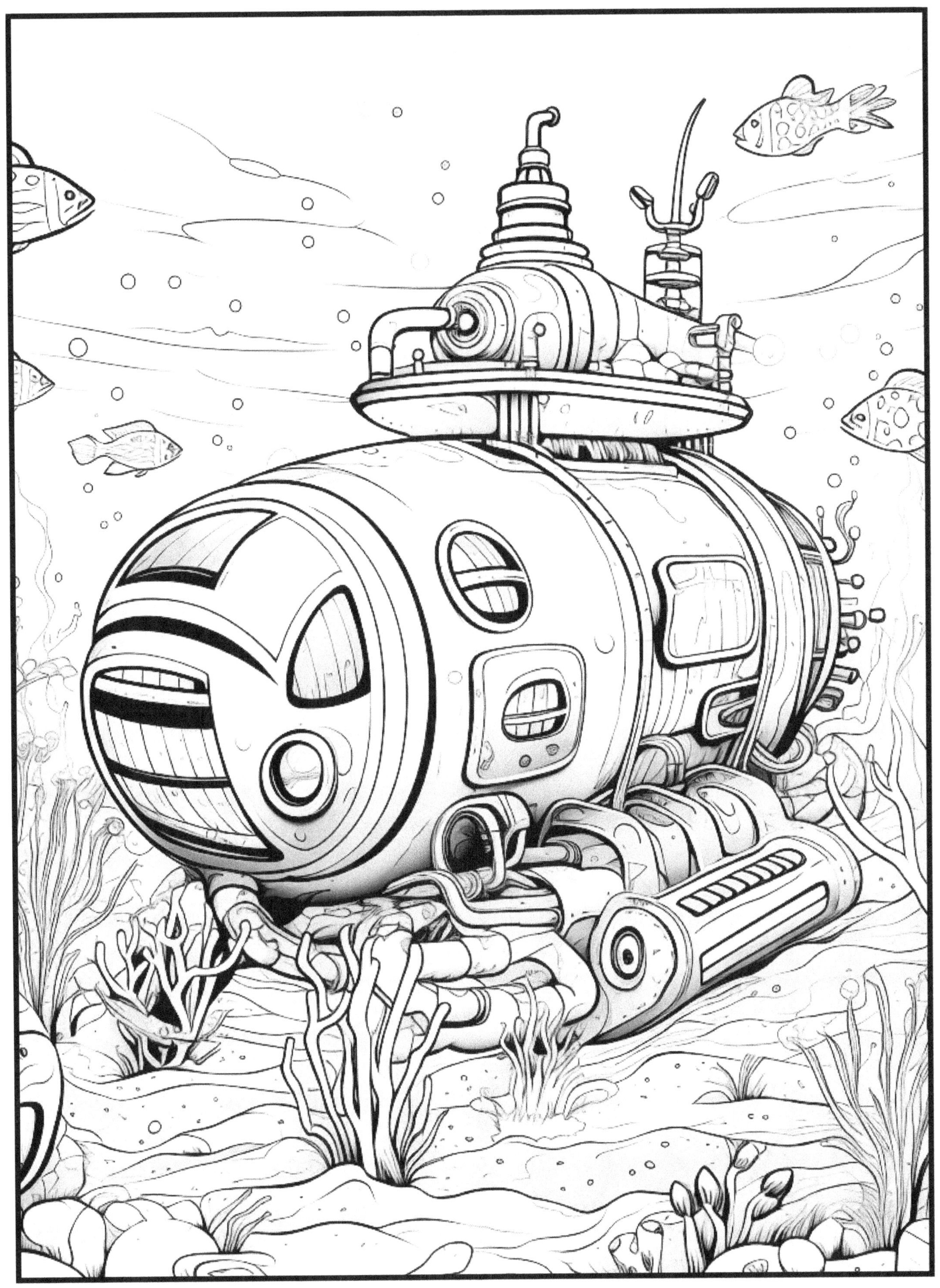

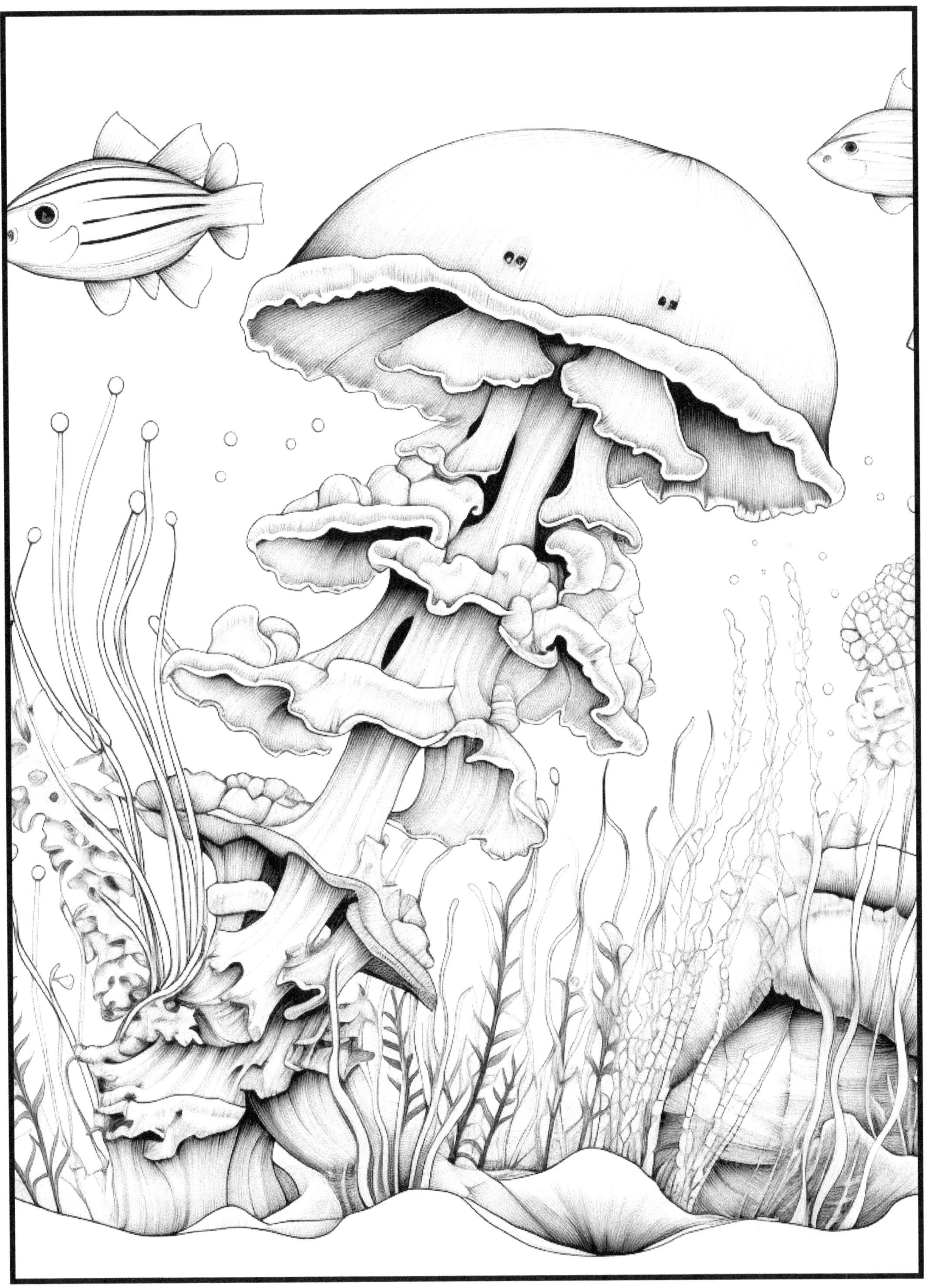

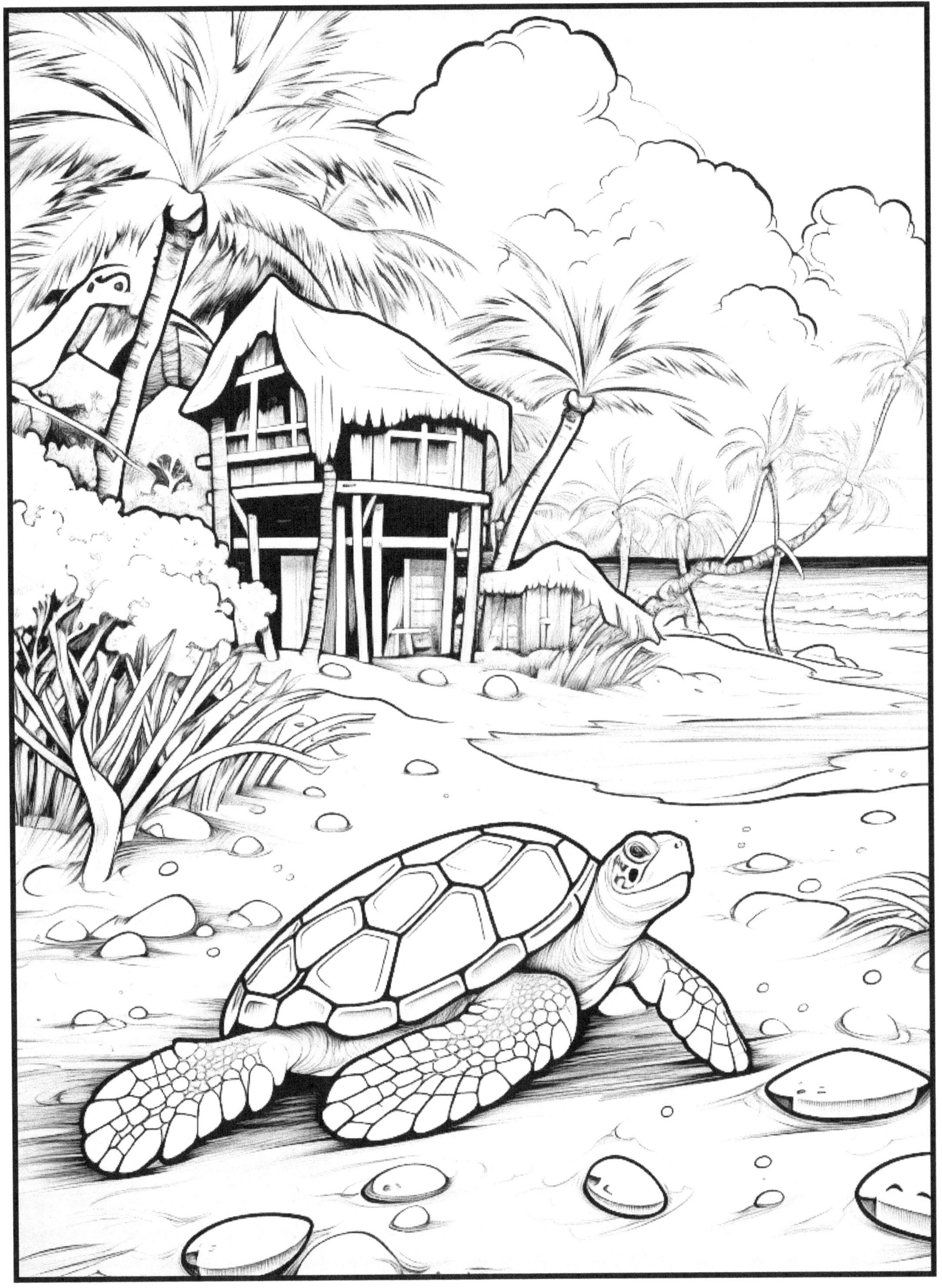

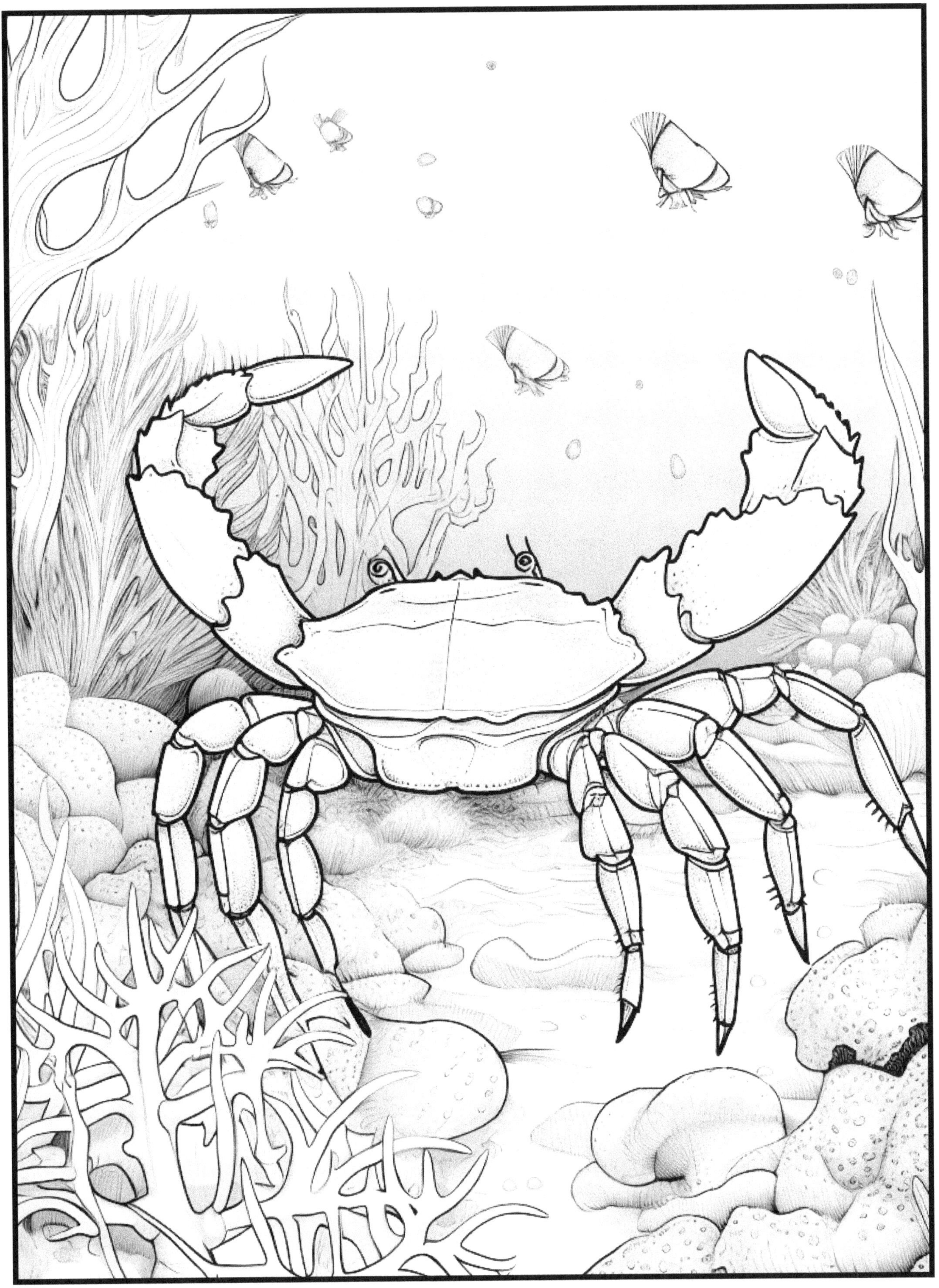

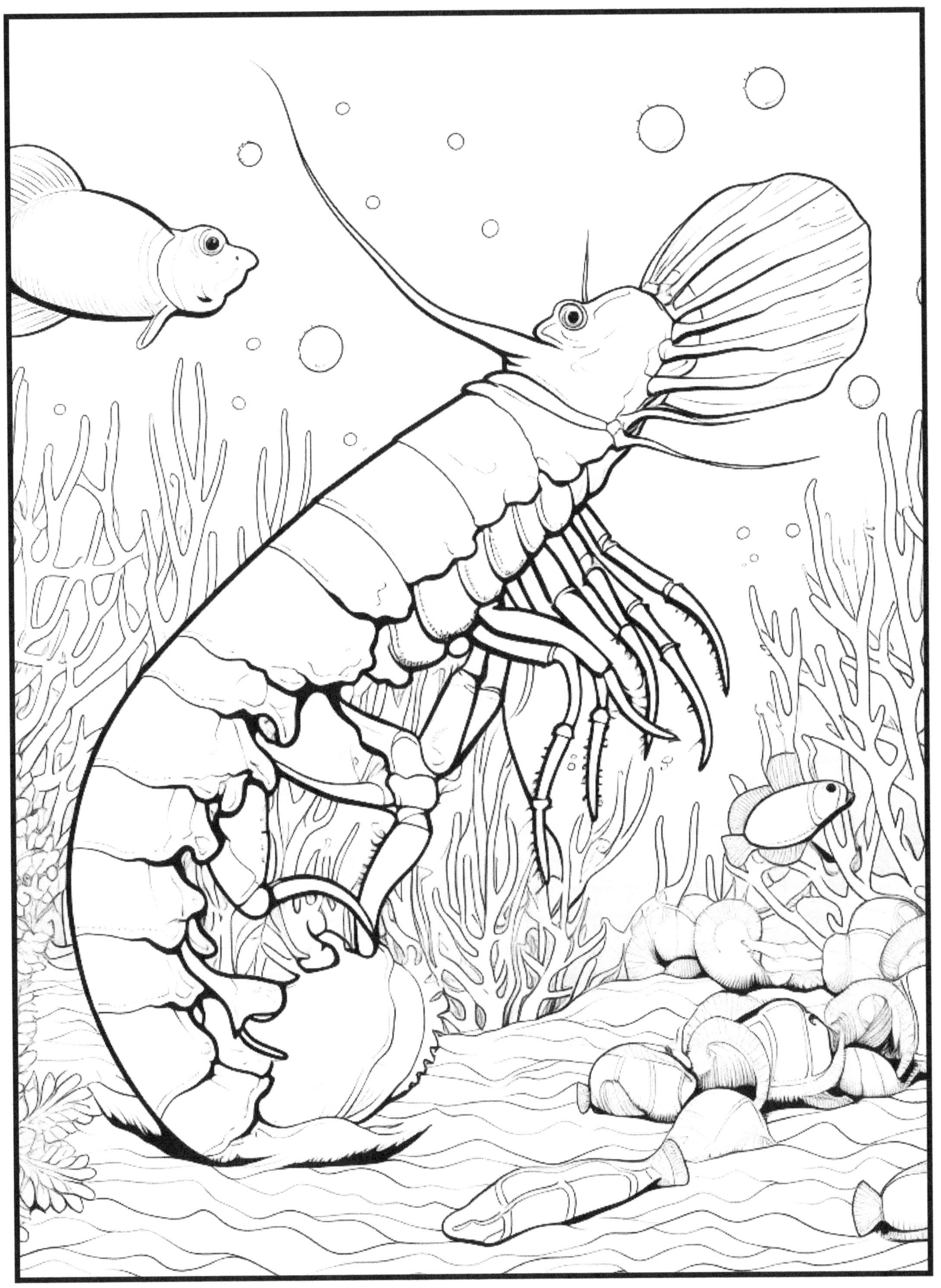

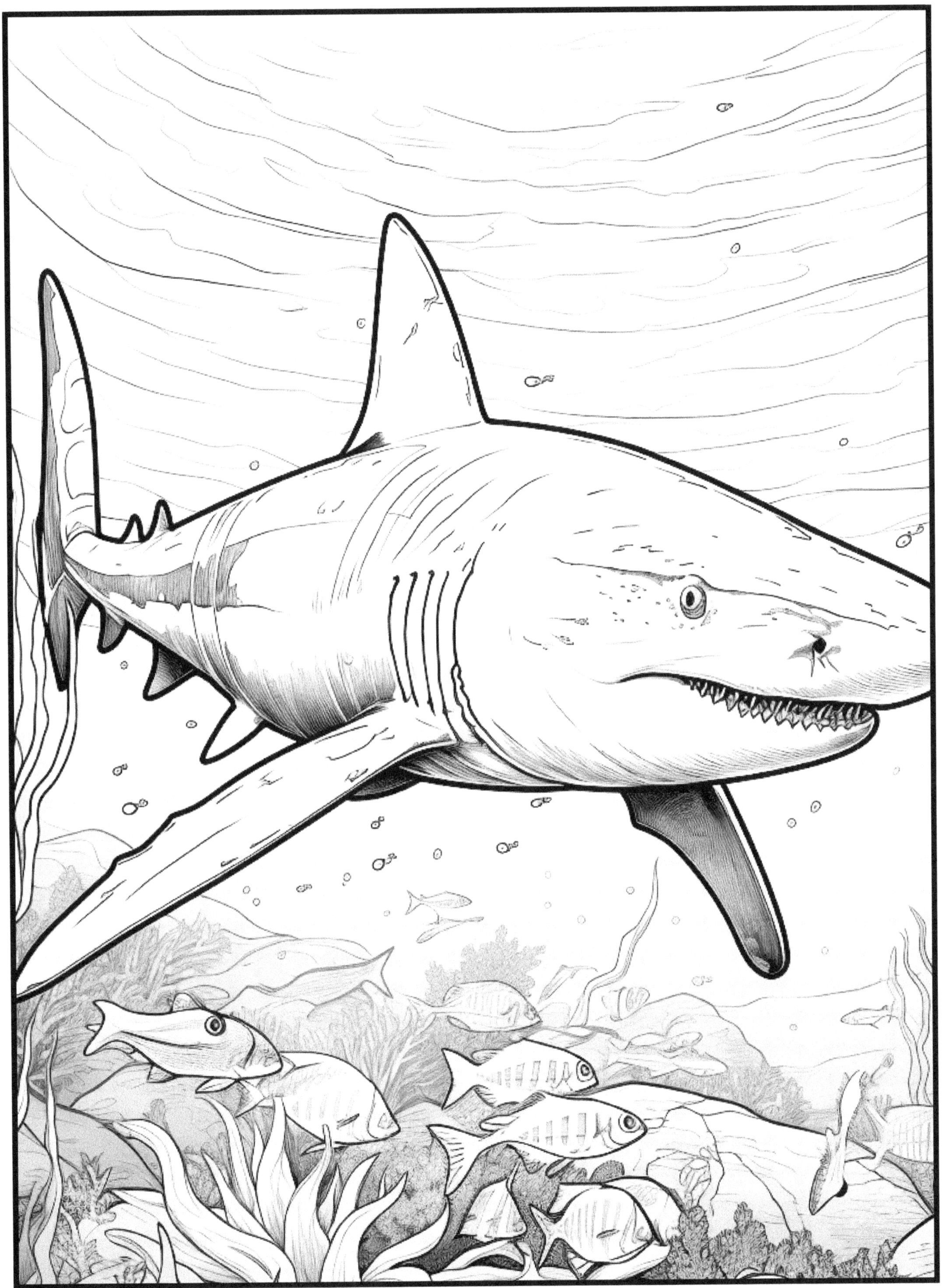

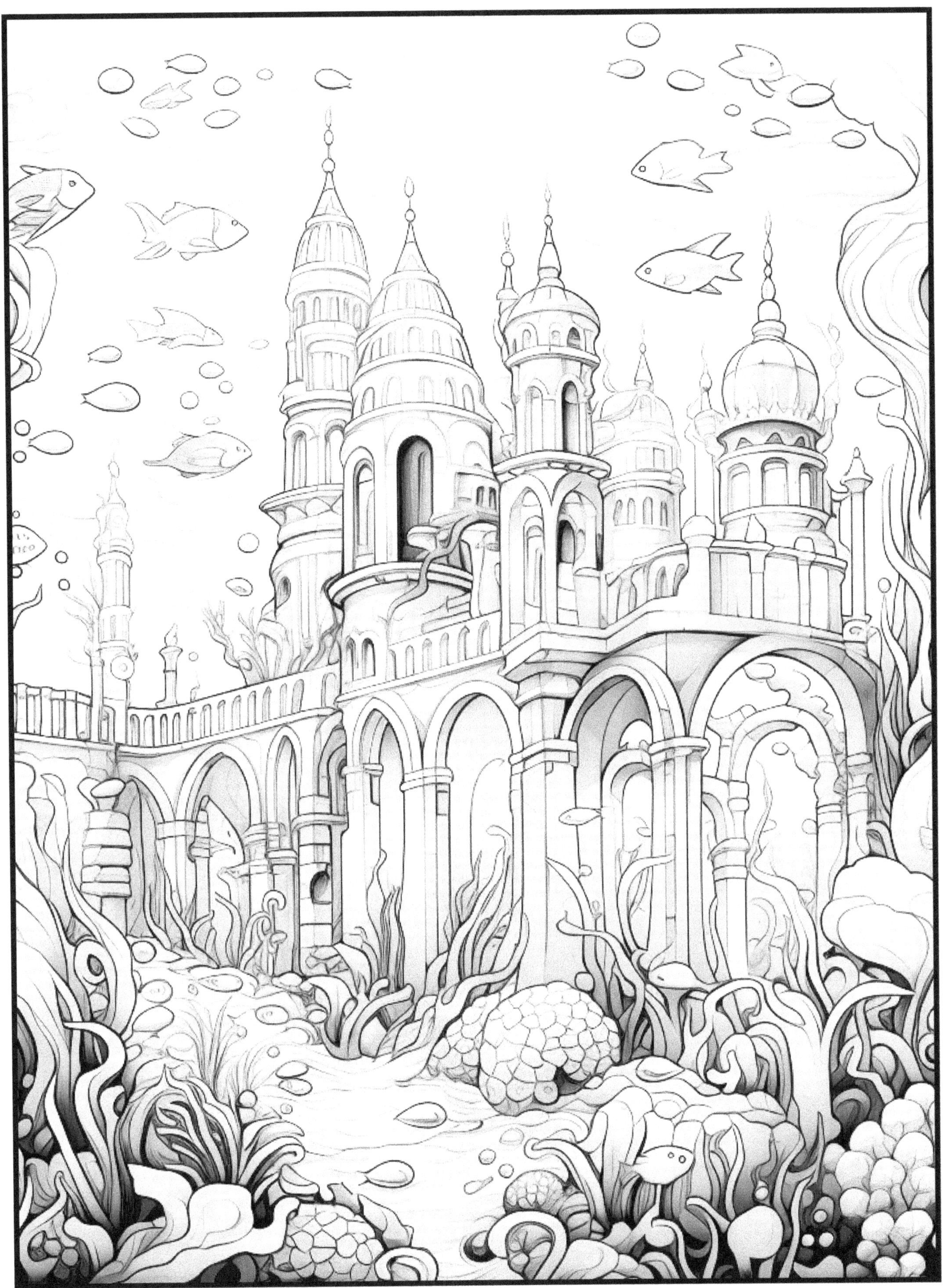

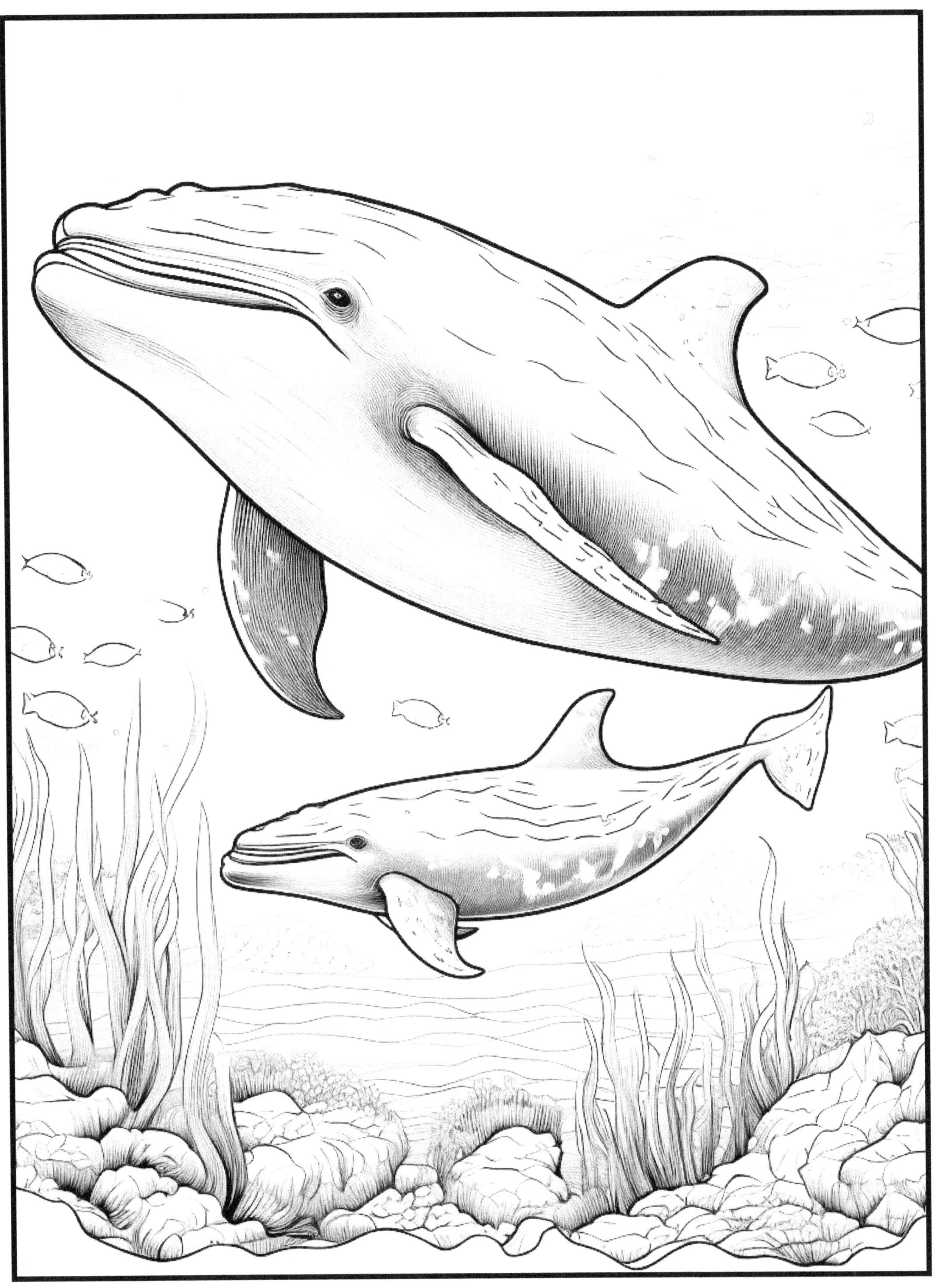

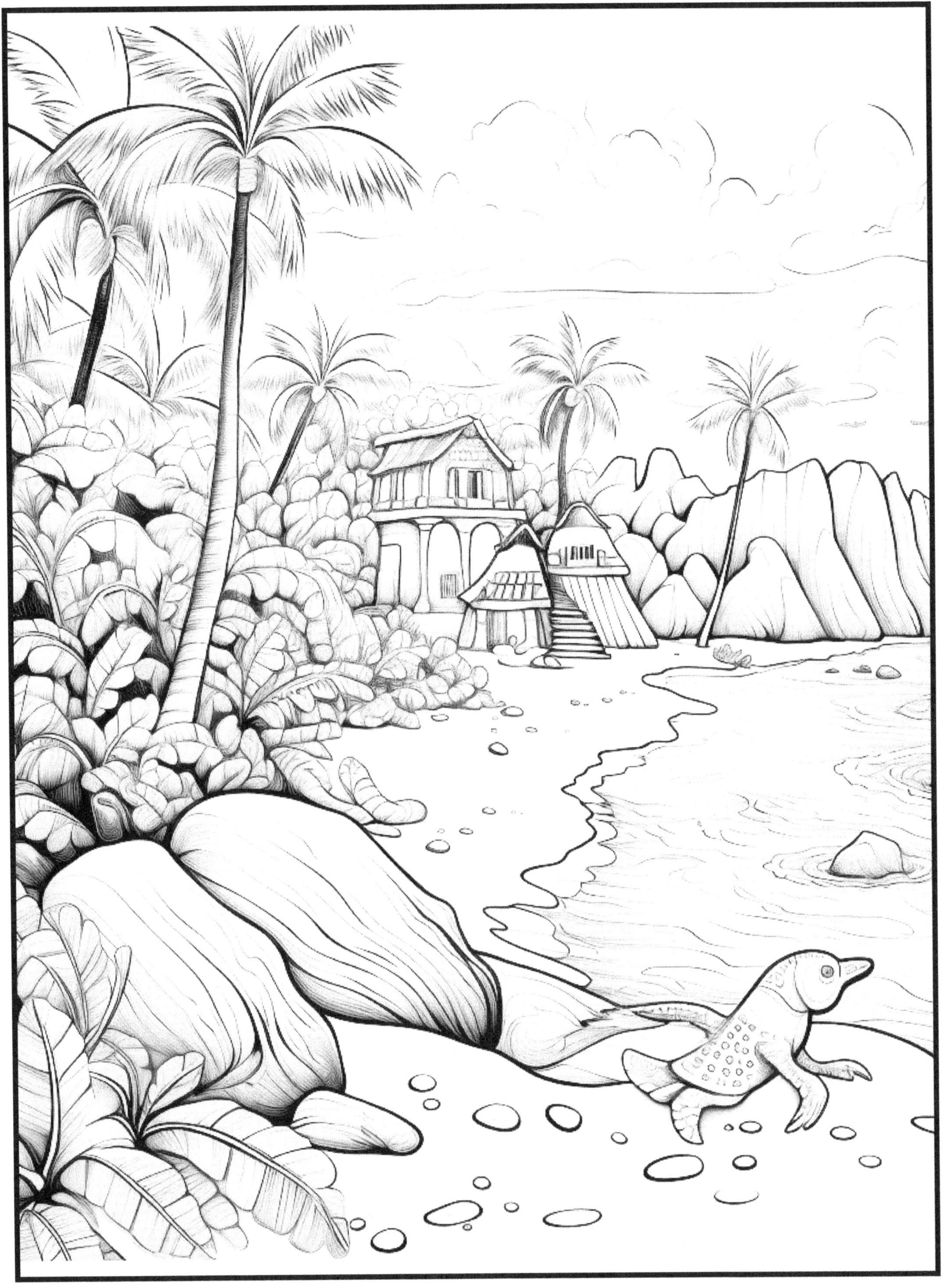

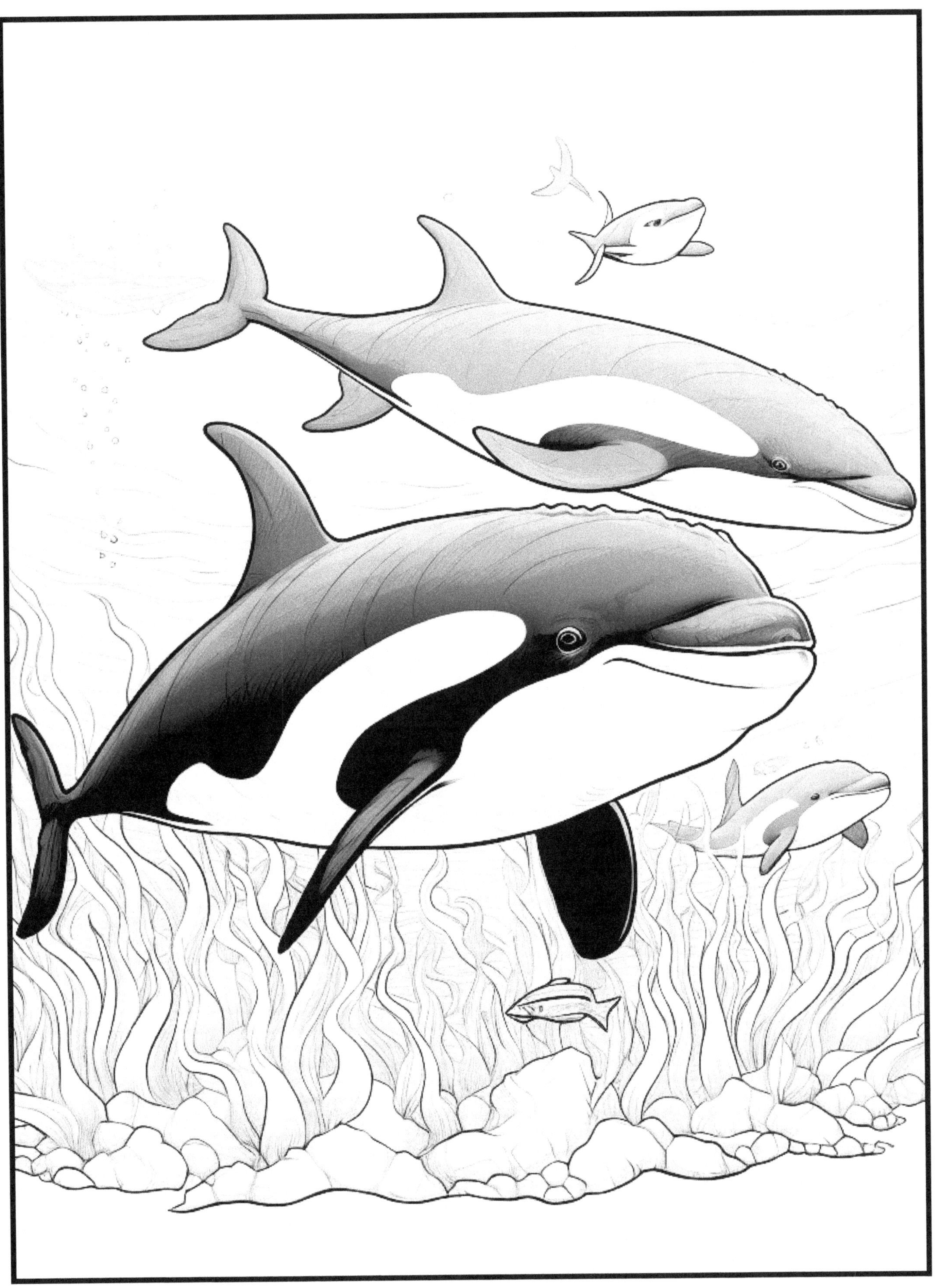